AuthorHouse™
1663 Liberty Drive
Bloomington, IN 47403
www.authorhouse.com
Phone: 1 (800) 839-8640

Published by AuthorHouse 03/31/2016

ISBN: 978-1-5049-8696-0 (sc)
ISBN: 978-1-5049-8697-7 (e)

Library of Congress Control Number: 2016904762

Print information available on the last page.

Any people depicted in stock imagery provided by Thinkstock are models,
and such images are being used for illustrative purposes only.
Certain stock imagery © Thinkstock.

This book is printed on acid-free paper.

authorHOUSE®

From the Heart

And Other Inspirational Poems

DIANA HUDSON

A True Friend

A person you cares about you when you're feeling bad,
Someone who comforts you when you're really sad.

A person who helps you through thick and thin,
And, always there when you need a friend.

A person who stand beside you, when no one else will,
Someone who understands, the way you feel.

You've been all the above,
given me strength, shown me love.

For all that you've been, all of my life,
Thank you for helping me find the truest friend, in my saviour, Jesus Christ.

Written by: Diana S. Hudson in 1982 for my best friend, Stephanie
O. Ward who moved to Lake Charles, Louisiana. Thank you Steph
for being my first best friend from Cord-Charlotte, Arkansas.

From The Heart

To my parents who I admire,

Who have a special quality that's hard to acquire.

Always being there through the years,

Despite the hardships, pain, and tears.

Before you, we'll soon stand,

Our diplomas, in our hands.

To you who have always cared,

This special time with you, shall soon be shared.

For all the wonderful things that you have done,

To make me feel like I was number one.

Thank you, from the bottom of my heart,

May no sadness, ever start.

The time has come, it's so near,

Tomorrow, graduation, will be here.

Taking a backwards glance,

Our memories, I now enhance.

Hurrying about---there's the cue,

All are ready, but a few.

Marching now, standing tall,

Oh, please, don't let me fall.

The excitement is hard to hide,

But, even more, is the nervousness inside.

Standing now, in a single line,

Our happiness, is undefined.

If it weren't for you, I'd be afraid,

But now, I've got it made.

Always there by my side,

Looking upon me now, with great pride.

For me you've always been there,

And, I want to say how much I care.

Mom and Dad, this is so true,

From the bottom of my heart---I Love You!

Written By: Diana S. Hudson May 25, 1985 (Read at our parent appreciation banquet, Published in our school annual with Our substituted for My and dedicated to all Our parents at Cord-Charlotte High School)

A New Day

What a glorious morning,

I am thankful for my life.

There's a coolness in the air,

That's opened my sleepy eyes.

As I take in this beauty--careful to observe,

I stand in awe of this planet Earth.

For what is a forest, without any trees?

Only a barren ground, brought to it's knees.

An ever-flowing river winds through the land,

My what an awesome world, from where I stand.

Over in the distance, a towering mountain climbs.

How could this mountain be, without the hand of time?

Without sediment, mud, and tiny pebbles,

This mighty mountain, would just be level.

Stunned by it's beauty, as the sun arises…

How could the sun exist without any skies?

Starting to rain now, the clouds descend.

Tell me, what is a cloud without any wind?

As the wind nudges the swaying trees,

I am refreshed by it's gentle breeze.

The slightest kisses of rain upon my face,

Carries my senses to a higher place.

Unmatched beauty--like a hand-sewn quilt,

I rest in blissfulness, without any guilt.

Surrounded by it's comfort--a pillow for my head…

I plunge into the depths of nature's feather bed.

Written by: Diana S. Hudson July 27, 1996

Sunset

As I sit on the rocks near the shore,

I can't remember feeling quite this way before.

All because of a marvelous sunset over the ocean,

Just within moments, all is in motion.

As the sun descends to say good-night…

A sea gull takes wing for one final breath-taking flight.

For the couples walking hand and hand,

This sunset has been especially planned.

One that they'll always want to remember,

One who's beauty has just begun to enter…

With a burst of colors the sky begins to change,

There's a hint of purple, a touch of pink, and an
accent of gold, entwined with orange.

Can you imagine such a spectacular sight?

The sun will tomorrow greet us once more, but for
now, winks good day and disappears

into the night.

With the lullaby of waves caressing against the shore,

And, a view like that, Who could ask for anything more?

Written By: Diana S. Hudson June 22, 1987

The Final Countdown

The time has come, countdown begins…
But, how were we to know that lives would end?

My, how magnificent the shuttle flew,
From where I stood it was a spectacular view.

All of America was watching, everyone was there,
But, no one suspected that death would soon linger in the air.

A Nation in waiting, with great anticipation,
And we never expected to witness devastation.

When the shuttle arose, there was excitement and cheers,
But what happened next, lead to rivers of tears…

For a moment, our lights from our hearts shone bright,
But in the next, something turned out the lights.

A flame appeared which seemed to be trouble,
And, it was that flame, which grew, to engulf the shuttle.

Stunned silence washed over us like a wave in the ocean,
Sadness, fear, disbelief, hope, a whole string of emotions…

It couldn't be happening, yet it was,
We were losing lives that were special to us.

In less than a heartbeat it came to a close,
How it happened? No one yet knows.

On the day of January 28, 1986,
Many hearts were broken, many feelings were mixed.

There was no warning to this great disaster,
But, America stood mourning for seven days after.

Many hearts are still yet weak,
But, there's still hope, still dreams to seek.

A journey which ended in reaching for the stars,
But, let's not give up, we still have our tomorrows.

Seven lives were taken away,
Yet, a million memories, in our hearts still stay.

It doesn't seem fair, what came to an end,
The loss of husbands, wives, children, and friends.

Yes, Challenger flew so proud and so high,
That no one knew it would end with Goodbye.

Now we realize there is no longer cause for alarm,
For our voyagers are safe in God's loving arms.

They have reached their last destination,
Their final countdown ending, to a teary-eyed nation.

Written By: Diana S. Hudson February 1, 1986

Thirty Pieces Of Silver

You've probably heard the story, It's often been told,

For thirty pieces of silver, Jesus was sold.

For this cruel act, Judas was to blame.

And, after he'd realized what he'd done, he hung himself in shame.

Thirty pieces of silver, it's an unworthy price for a life to be paid.

But, it was enough for Judas at the time he'd betrayed.

No He couldn't deny what he had done.

For thirty pieces of silver, he sold God's only Son.

When he saw the harm he'd caused, he tossed the bag aside.

But, it wasn't enough to rid him of the guilt burning inside.

And, it came to pass…

The moment had arrived.

The time had come, for Jesus to be crucified.

I can imagine, what Judas must have felt, as time crept slowly by.

He thought, "Why must it have to be me?" "Why, Dear Lord?" "Why?"

"This was not a worthy price…"

"To pay for Jesus, The one who is truly Christ…"

"How could I have done such a cruel, and worthless deed?"

"How could I just stand back, and watch my Savior bleed?"

"Father, forgive me, my crime can not be undone."

"But, I'll never forget, that I denied your Son."

Thirty pieces of silver, it bought Jesus, this is true.

But, it can't pay for what He did for me and you…

Thirty pieces of silver, for the one from above,

It will never pay for His grace, or His everlasting love…

Written By : Diana S. Hudson April 17, 1987

Can You Believe?

Can you believe that God created all things?
He did.

In the petals of an orchid, His delicate handiwork can be seen.
He made all, from the mightiest oceans, to the smallest of trickling streams.

From the wind that whispers through the gently swaying trees,
To the magnificent splendor of the colorful, dancing autumn leaves.

You can experience the endless beauty in both a sunrise and sunset.
Did God create these things? Yes, indeed! On that, you can bet.

You can look up in the sky, on a clear dark night,
And gaze. at the countless number of stars, that shine so bright.

From the emerald green pastures, to the crystal blue sky,
God has created all that surrounds us, just for you and I.

Can you believe that He has always been around?
From everlasting, to everlasting, His love will forever abound.

Can you believe that this and so much more is waiting just for you?
God created rainbows, sunshine, golden meadows, and early morning dew.

He's given us so many precious gifts to be with us everywhere.
But, the most precious gift of all, really shows how much He cares.

He sent His only Son to die for our sins.
And, for this we praise Him. Our hearts, overflowing from within.

The most wonderful gift of all, is easy to receive,
Just give you heart to God, and truly believe.

Written by Diana Hudson January 24, 1988

Open Your Heart To Me
—Stranger On A Park Bench

There you are just sitting there,

Feeling alone, like no one cares.

You've kept all your emotions inside.

But, now, they're much harder to hide.

All is not right, all is not well,

But, just looking at you, that's easy to tell.

You've searched your soul, found the disease,

And, now, it's time to seek inner peace.

So, listen to me, come sit by my side,

Tell me of your troubles, and swallow that pride.

Open your heart, let me inside,

For your sins, you cannot hide.

What is this? You're scared, you say?

Take my hand, I'll lead the way…

Open your heart, give me the key,

Open your heart, for this is my plea.

You're not alone; I've always been there,

And, I'm here now, to show you I care.

So let me know how much you're hurting down deep,

For when you are sorrowed, I silently weep.

Open your heart, it's for you I wait.

Let me inside, right now. Before it's too late.

Open your heart, let the sun shine in.

Open your heart, let me wash away all the sin.

Open your heart, Let me fill it with love,

For I am the Son of God from above.

Open your heart, and you will be free.

Open your heart, open it, to me.

Written By: Diana S. Hudson 1987

Glistening Falls

Ever since I was small,

I've had a fascination with waterfalls.

Their brilliance cascading down,

More beautiful than a golden crown.

An essence that takes my breath away,

Here by the falls is where I long to stay.

I love to see the foamy waves,

And long to explore some of their hidden caves.

Their waters glistening in the sun,

Like a spider's web that has just been spun.

I love to feel their misty spray,

As once again, my breath is taken away.

It doesn't matter if it's night or day,

They're ever-flowing in their magnificent array.

Yes, loving nature is the thing you see,

So, when you see a waterfall, remember me.

Written By: Diana S. Hudson June 5, 1997

A Thanksgiving Prayer

Our gracious heavenly father, who painted the skies above,

And created this world for us with His guidance and His love.

We thank thee, Lord, for such a beautiful day…

That we'd be blessed, as we take this time out, to pray.

May all our loved ones be close today, not a single one out of touch,

And may all of those who have gone astray, left
your service, lost their way, may they

find you for it means so much.

Bless this time, with our neighbors and friends,

For we hope, that this day never, ever ends…

Thank you, for this day we share,

Showing others, how much we care.

Bless each one so dear,

Who has made this day special by just being here.

We thank thee, Lord, for a love so kind,

That without your grace, we could not find.

O' Lord we thank thee from our hearts so deep, so filled with love,

For this day so full of warmth, and joy, and
wonderful feelings, and for the comfort in

knowing your gracious love.

Bless this day O' Lord we pray,

May we feel it's meaning in so many ways.

Bless our friends whose love will be shared,

As we partake in a feast with much love prepared.

May this Thanksgiving be filled with love so true,

For my dearest Lord, we love you.

May each day be better than the last,

And, make sweetest memories of Thanksgiving's past.

Dear Lord, O' how you've made my life so worth living.

For all of these things, we ask in your name,
Amen, and Happy Thanksgiving!

Written By: Diana S. Hudson November 23, 1986

Give Your Heart o God

If you're feeling tired,

If you're feeling weary,

If you're feeling sad,

Or feeling blue…

You don't have to fret,

You don't have to worry,

Cause I've got the answer for you…

Give your heart to God,

Give your soul to Jesus,

Let Him fill you up with His love…

Give your heart to God,

Give your soul to Jesus,

Feel the cleansing power of His blood…

Someday soon I will meet my maker,

Someday soon so will you…

I know of His love,

I know of His power,

And, if you'll try, so can you…

Give your heart to God,

Give your soul to Jesus,

Let Him feel you up with His love…

Give your heart to God,

Give your soul to Jesus,

Feel the cleansing power of His blood…

No more are you tired,

No more are you weary,

No more are you sad,

Or feeling blue…

Just listen to your heart,

It will tell you clearly,

To serve the Lord, here's what you do…

Give your heart to God,

Give your soul to Jesus,

Let Him feel you up with His love…

Give your heart to God,

Give your soul to Jesus,

Feel the cleansing power of His blood…

Written as song for my mom, Shirley Jane Milligan
Manuel By: Diana S. Hudson 1987

How Do You See Jesus?

Do you see Jesus as a babe, wrapped in swaddling
clothes, lying in a manger, filled with hay?

Or, do you see him as a small boy, in His father's carpenter
shop, where He Learned to work, day by day?

Do you see Him, as the one who faced the temptations
of satan, and mastered them all?

Or, perhaps you see Him, as the one who performed
miracles, none of which were small?

Maybe you see Him as The Good Shepherd, who
saved the lamb, that went astray?

But, do you see Him, as the one who fills your life everyday?

Do you see Him, riding into Jerusalem, upon a colt?

The Messiah, who came to them, bringing forth, great hope.

Can you imagine, how He felt, at The Last Supper,
when He knew, He had been betrayed?

Can you see Him, in The Garden, of Gethsemane, kneeling, as He prayed?

I see Jesus,dressed in a scarlet robe, bearing a crown of thorns upon
His head, being mocked, spit upon, by many, savage men.

They did not even realize, or care, that it was
He, who was dying, for their sins.

Then, I see Jesus, bearing the cross, up a hill, called Calvary.

For this, is where, He died, to save, you and me.

I see the Roman soldiers, stretching Jesus out, upon the
cross, and nailing Him, to it's wooden beams.

I can feel, His agony, as the rusty nails, are tearing,
through His flesh, yet, He didn't even scream.

Do you see Him, dying, slowly, nailed to the cross?

He was innocent, but, for our sins, He paid the cost.

I see Him, as my King, who finally cried, "It's
finished", Yet, it, had only, begun

I see Him, as God's perfect Son.

I feel, His presence, not just here, but, in every place.

I can feel, His mighty power, His love and His grace.

I see Jesus, as my saviour, who died, and, then arose.

I see His handiwork, in, a single, perfect rose.

I see Jesus, as the one, who will, come again.

I see Jesus, as the friend, of every man.

Do you, see Jesus, in any, of these ways?

Are you, in His service,? Do you, give Him, praise?

I still picture Jesus, nailed to the cross.

For without Him, in my life, I would be lost.

Do you really realize for you all He has done?

And, if you just let Him, into your life, that, He's only, just begun.

I see Jesus, with His, ever extended hand.

I see Jesus, reaching out, not to one, but every man.

I see Jesus, each time, I bow, to pray.

I see Jesus, in my life, everyday.
I see Him, as the one, who catches me, when I fall.

I see Him, as my, all in all.

How do You see Jesus? Do you see Him in these ways?

Do you know His love? Have you experienced His grace?

How do you see Jesus? I, ask you, today?

Because, I know, that if we only ask Him, our sins, He will erase.

Written by: Diana S. Hudson March 1987

As I Recall, Days of Yesteryear

As I recall, days of yesteryear,
I remember days filled with love, and laughter. Not much sorrow, or tears.

I remember those days of Spring,
When life begins to grow into everything.

The sunny meadows, the clear blue sky,
The fresh-baked smell of moma's blackberry pie.

The wind blowing it's gentle breeze,
As it nudged the branches of the big oak trees.

We'd work all day til the chores were done,
And after supper, Papa would play the fiddle and we'd have some fun.

Then we'd say our prayers and to bed we'd go,
Because come sunrise, that old cock would sure enough crow.

Then came the dewy morning,
When flowers would smile at you without any warning.

Us young folk would walk to school without fail,
And we'd carry our lunch in our old, tin pails.

Papa would work all through the week,
Just so we all could make ends meet.

Then on Sunday the church bell would ring,
Down in the valley, over the hills, you could hear its echoes sing.

I remember our silver-haired preacher man,
His soft-spoken ways, and his strong, firm, hands.

He spoke so proud and so bold,
And, from his lips the stories of the Bible were told.

I remember the trickling streams,
The leaves of Autumn, and the wintry evergreens.

I wish I could bring those days back here,
But, as I recall, those are now fondest memories, of yesteryear.

Written By: Diana S. Hudson April 17,1987

Let Freedom Ring

On July 4, 1776, Our freedom began…

Freedom for an independent land.

Thirteen colonies were declared to be free,

Looking toward a future filled with hope and much prosperity.

Ah, Freedom! Something we all seem to take for granted,

But, in the midst of those colonies, is where freedom was planted.

Freedom was gently and so lovingly sewn into our
American flag. Yes, in each thread of

red, white, and blue.

Freedom waves each day in salute to those who've
fought and died to keep it for me and

you.

The red stands for the blood of our fellow countrymen
who carry these scars still today,

of battles both won and lost.

For those who've bravely fought to keep the freedom,
to us should be so much, that with

their lives they paid the cost.

The white stands for hope and faith of a land where the future shines bright..

The stars represent each of the 50 states, and the
blue stands for the sky in a pool of

midnight.

The Declaration of Independence, Our Constitution,
Lady Liberty, The Liberty Bell, and

"A Star Spangled Celebration" stand for freedom but, not alone...

Our faith, hope, and dreams with these belong.

Together with our high flying flag, they all
represent on very important thing,

As each year we celebrate Our Nation's Birthday,

Let us hear freedom ring.

Written By: Diana S. Hudson July 2, 1987

A Christmas Wish

At this special time of year,

We think of happiness, joy, and cheer.

A special time we share with friends,

A kind of magic we hope won't end.

A time for giving, a time to share,

A time to spread our love everywhere.

So, reach out and touch a hand,

For peace on Earth, throughout the land.

Bringing joy to you as it may,

Remembering the joy of Christ's birthday.

A time to love, a time to share,

A time to show how much we care.

Remember the mange where He lay,

The Lord Jesus, asleep on the hay.

Remember His life that He gave,

For our souls He did save.

Remember the blood upon His hands,

So here today, with you I stand.

So what is my Christmas wish, you ask?

It's really simple, not a hard task.

Let the special warmth in the air,

Fill your heart, and linger there.

And, if you believe in Christmas magic, (which I do),

Hold the hand of someone next to you.

Make them your new friend on this day,

For peace begins in this way.

And, If you believe in it too,

Be my friend, I'll be yours too. Merry Christmas and God bless you!

Written By: Diana S. Hudson 1985

A Soldier's Prayer

Dear Heavenly Father, Please Hear my cry,
For, I am a soldier Lord, and wounded am I.

I've been hit really hard, and brought down fast.
Please help me make it Lord, don't let this prayer be my last.

I've always known you were close by my side.
You've heard me in laughter, held me when I cried.

The skies are darkened now, but the explosions are almost blinding it seems.
The roar of thunder from plane engines: the sounds of war, are deafening.

Sirens of air raid, missiles aflame,
I know I will never be the same.

I miss my family, and loved ones back home.
And, I know Lord, that I am not alone.

Still, I can't help myself, from being afraid.
That's why I've come to you tonight, and prayed.

So help me, if you will, by giving me the courage
and endurance, to withstand.
Open my eyes to hope, and supply me with
inner peace, so I might understand.

Why must this fighting rage on?
Help me stand,for what's right, til the battle's won!

Shelter me, in a blanket of faith, with your arms of love.
I need your guidance, my dear Father, from above.

Although, I've been struck, with such an impact,
Help me, turn the other cheek, and not my back.

I don't want to die, on this foreign soil,
Among all the confusion,fear, and turmoil.

Please be with the leader's of our world and nation.
Don't let us end up in total devastation.

Help us all, to have faith, and believe.
May you will,be done, in every deed.
Fill our hearts, with the strength, and love we need.

My prayer is that each soldier not be alone.
And, If we don't make it back alive, Lord, then we are still,coming home.

Although I,ve not yet been harmed in a physical way,
Stress,confusion, frustration,anxiety, my emotions, are being held at bay.

There may be that time to come when I can no longer stand.
If that time does come, may I breathe my last breath,
with dignity, honor, and I, at your command.

Written By: Diana S. Hudson in the wake of Desert
storm. Dedicated to all, who serve our military.

Eva's Song

So many times I've seen myself stumble,
Hoping to capture that ring of brass.

And, there are times my heart's been humbled,
Walking through pastures, of daisies and grass.

And, He has always been there,
To carry me along.
He is the one that I can cling to,
When faced with life's storms.

Through His strength,
Through infinite wisdom,
He guides me on my way.
Holding me steady---not to sway.

And, He--He is the light,
That chases the shadows away.
He is the one,
That carries me on,
Day by day.

Written By: Diana S. Hudson June 22,1996 (For my good
friend, and co-worker Eva Kruse) Thanks for the inspiration.

Just A Simple Man

God gave me the talent to build with my own hands,

A home for my family--it was part of His plan.

He's given me a good wife, a daughter, and a son.

Blessings all around me, and He's only just begun.

I'm not a rich man.

Pretty down to earth.

But, I give my all to Jesus, because my all is what He's worth.

I don't have to have many things,

I could live off the land.

But, I couldn't survive without His guiding hand.

My wife stands beside me whatever I may do,

My children give me lots of pride, and lots of laughter too.

I'm just a simple man.

Pretty down to earth.

But, I give my all to Jesus, because my all is what He's worth.

God gave me compassion to help those in need,

No matter what the tragedy, I go where He leads.

I've been blessed with lots of friends, and a sense of humor too.

You ask me how I'm blessed? It's all in attitude.

I'm a very lucky man.

Humble, down to earth.

And, I give my all to Jesus, because my all is what He's worth.

Written By: Diana S. Hudson June 23, 1996 (Inspired by a good friend and his family, may you always be richly blessed.)

A Word of Prayer

When our hearts are filled with love,
For our Father, from above.

In times of joy, throughout the year;
In times of laughter, in times of tears,

When often there are sorrows shared,
Let us have a word of prayer.

As our hearts cry out, for those in pain,
Let us pray, again, and again.

For those who are yet unsaved; who need our Savior's cleansing blood,
May we pray, that they receive, His everflowing flood.

In times of happiness, in times of cheer,
Let us praise Him so all may hear.

As we fellowship,with each other,
Let us remember, all our brothers.

Those who are sad, or may be ill,
Let us show them, how we feel.

As we pray, at the altar,
May we pray, that no one falters.

May each knee bend,
As we pray, for every friend.

For each one, express our love,
And thank God, from above.

As we pray let's join hands,
For peace, throughout our world's lands.

Remember our pastor, and his wife.
Remember Jesus, who gave His life.

Remember our families whose love we share,
Let them know, how much we care.

Let us rid ourselves of all our fears, worry, and tension.
Yet, remember His love, so great, that words, can hardly mention.

And, when we see someone, who needs a friend,
Let us be there, for them, to the end.

For everyone, and everything,
Let each heart, His praises, sing.

For all of those, whose lives, we share,
Let us have, a word of prayer.

Written by: Diana S. Hudson. April 13, 1987

The Prettiest Rose

Each and every morning she had her daily routine..

She would step out on her porch and listen to the birds sing.

She'd look toward the eastern sky and greet the rising sun.

Then she'd walk among the roses…

It was how her day begun.

She'd slip one in her fingers and feel its velvet touch…

These are life's little treasures she enjoyed so much.

She'd kneel a little closer and take a deep breath of air…

She was taking in their fragrance…

And, it was everywhere.

Among her roses is where she felt her best…

Among her roses she felt so blessed.

Every morning Buck and I would travel down
the pathway to say "Good Morning

Mama"…

(He's my shadow, that big, brown, dog)

She'd raise her head and turn to greet us before
we'd get halfway, and smile, "Good

Morning Son"…

Her parakeet would see us and warn her with his calls.

(He was her protection, that tiny, green, bird)

We'd walk for awhile and see if each other needed anything…

Then she'd say "Son, have you seen my roses
lately?" And, she'd hum and sing.

Among her roses we began to walk,

And, I listened to her wisdom, as she began to talk.

Son, here stands a special bush almost eight feet tall..

A bud has snuck through the spaces of the lattice wall.

And, it greets me each morning, the first one of all.

It's petals are crimson red and it's leaves are dark green…

Among all my roses, it's the prettiest I've seen.

This is the rose that Heaven's angels have kissed…

This is my rose of Happiness.

And, today, although she peacefully sleeps…

I know, that she knows, in her hands we placed "that" rose

Just so she could see it every morning, as she walks with her best friend.

Written By: Diana S. Hudson

In Memory of : A Very Special Lady…My
Grandmother (Ma) Noma E. Staggs Manuel

She still watches over me…

Printed in the United States
By Bookmasters